SCHIRMER'S LIBRARY
OF MUSICAL CLASSICS

JOSEPH HAYDN

Twenty Sonatas

For the Piano

Edited and Fingered by

LUDWIG KLEE and DR. SIGMUND LEBERT

Book I contains a Biographical Sketch of the Author by

DR. THEODORE BAKER

IN TWO BOOKS

Book I (Nos. 1-10) — Library Vol. 295

→ Book II (Nos. 11-20) — Library Vol. 296

ISBN 0-7935-0770-7

G. SCHIRMER, Inc.

DISTRIBUTED BY

Hal•Leonard®
CORPORATION

7777 W. BLUEMOUND RD. P.O. BOX 13819 MILWAUKEE, WI 53213

Index.

Vol. II.

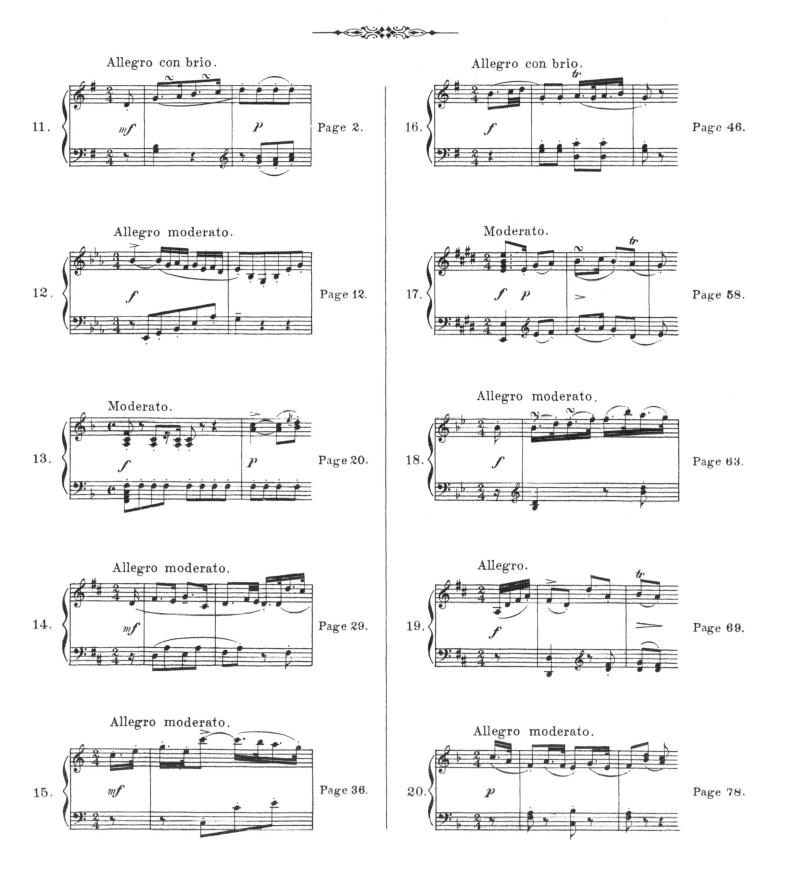

SONATA.

Abbreviations: *) M. T. signifies Main Theme; Ep., Episode; S.T., Sub-Theme; Cl.T., Closing Theme; D. G., Development-group; Md. T., Mid-Theme; R., Return; Tr., Transition; Cod., Codetta; I, II, III signify 1st, 2nd, and 3rd parts of a movement in song-form (Liedform).

Allegro con brio. (♩ = 116.)

JOSEPH HAYDN.

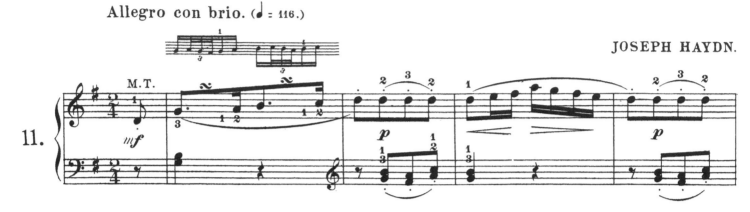

*) German equivalents: M. T. signifies Hauptsatz; Ep., Zwischensatz; S.T., Seitensatz; Cl.T., Schlusssatz; D.G., Durchführungssatz; Md.T., Mittelsatz; R., Rückgang; Tr., Übergang; Cod., Anhang; I. II. III., 1., 2. u. 3. Theil eines liedförmigen Satzes.

a) In the original edition, these four 32nd notes are marked as follows, throughout the movement:

b)

a) In the original, mordents are given here; but inverted mordents are doubtless intended.
b) After the hold, a slight pause should be made.

Menuetto. (♩ = 108.)

a) These turns always fall on the last note of the accompaniment-figure; in this case, therefore, on the third note of the second beat.
b) Continue without further pause.

11705

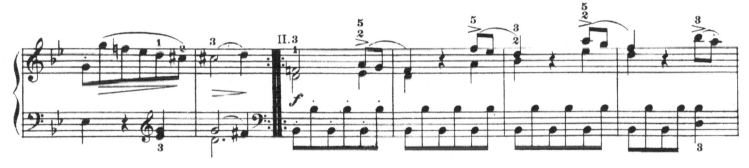

Trio.

Menuetto D.C.

a)   b)   c) As at b).

11705

Theme.

Presto. ($\flat$ = 152.)

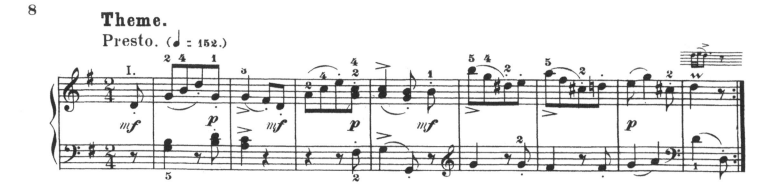

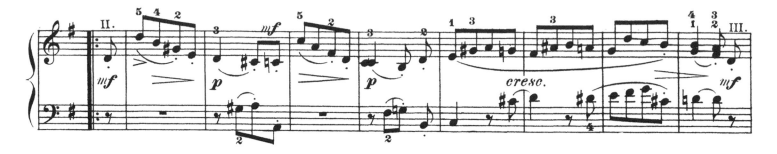

Var. I.

Var. II.

Var. III.

Var. IV.

11705

SONATA.

Abbreviations: M.T. signifies Main Theme; Ep., Episode; S.T., Sub-Theme; Cl.T., Closing Theme; D.G., Development-group; Md.T., Mid-Theme; R., Return; Tr., Transition; Cod., Codetta; I, II, III, 1st, 2nd, and 3rd parts of a movement in song-form (Liedform).

Revised and Fingered by
LUDWIG KLEE.

JOSEPH HAYDN.

Copyright, 1894, by G. Schirmer, Inc.

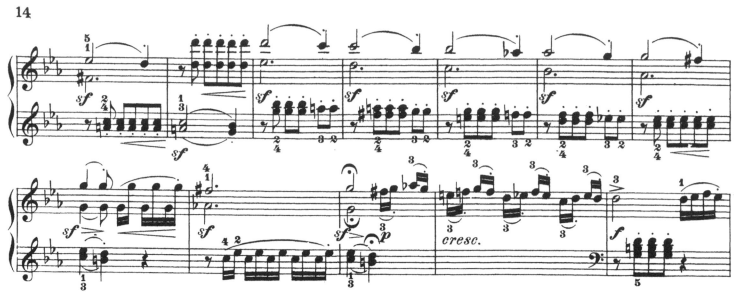

Menuetto.

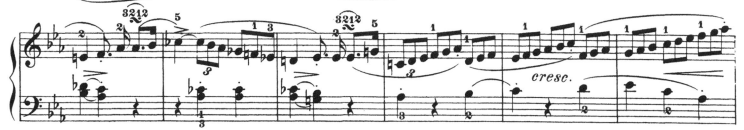

Trio.

Men. D. C.

Presto.

Var. I.

Var. II.

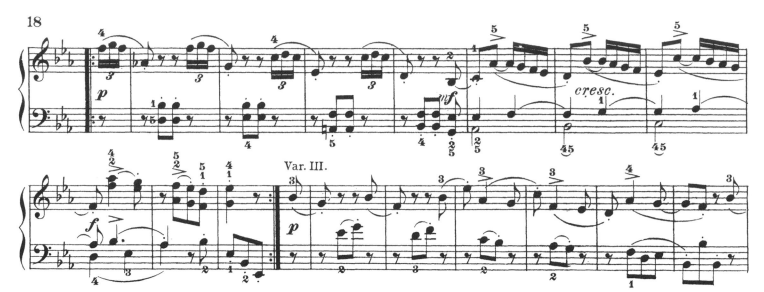

Var. III.

Var. IV.

a)

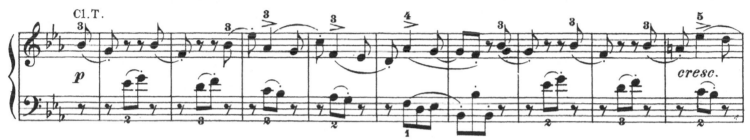

SONATA.

Abbreviations: M.T. signifies Main Theme; Ep., Episode; S.T., Sub-Theme; Cl.T., Closing Theme; D.G., Development-group; I, II, III signify 1st, 2nd, and 3rd parts of a movement in song-form.(Liedform.)

Revised and fingered by
LUDWIG KLEE.

JOSEPH HAYDN.

Copyright, 1894, by G. Schirmer, Inc.

23

11707

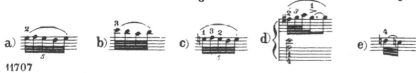

Tempo di Menuetto.

Minore.

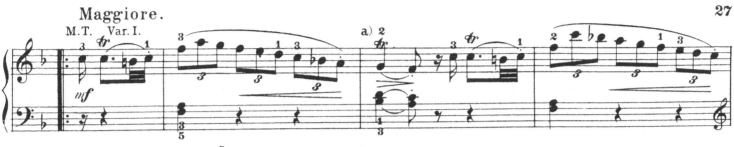

Maggiore.

a) easier: b) As at a)

11707

27

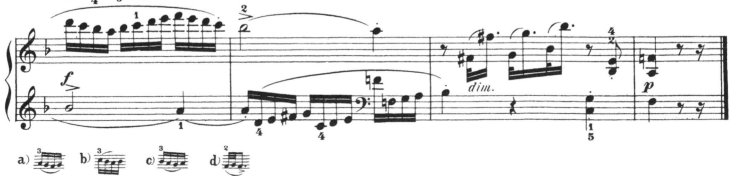

SONATA.

Abbreviations: M. T. signifies Main Theme; Ep., Episode; S. T., Sub-Theme; Cl. T., Closing Theme; D. G., Development-Group; Cod., Codetta; I, II, and III, 1st, 2nd, and 3rd parts of a movement in song-form (Liedform).

Revised and Fingered by
LUDWIG KLEE.

J. HAYDN.

Allegro moderato.

Menuetto.

Trio.

a) easier: b) easier: c) d) easier: e) like b. f) g) h) like d. i) like h.

Menuetto D. C.

Presto.

D.G.

legato.

a)

11708

SONATA.

Abbreviations: M. T. signifies Main Theme; Ep., Episode; S. T., Sub-Theme; Cl. T., Closing Theme; D. G., Development-Group.

Revised and Fingered by
LUDWIG KLEE.

J. HAYDN.

Allegro moderato.

15.

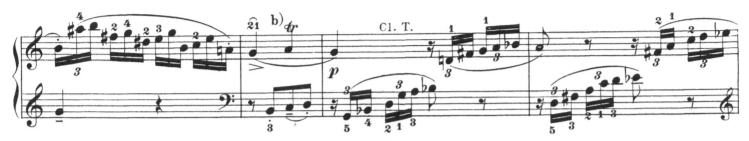

11709

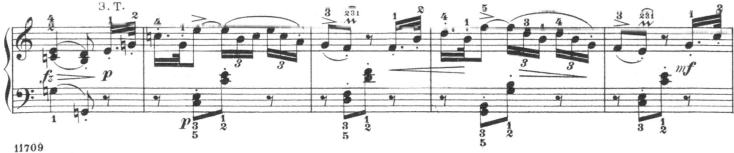

Adagio.

Finale.
Presto.

a)   b) like a)   c)

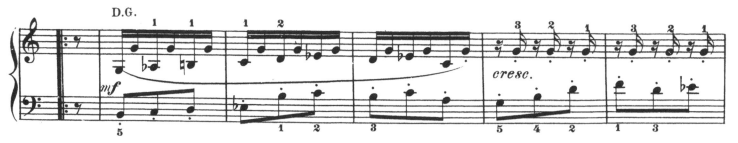

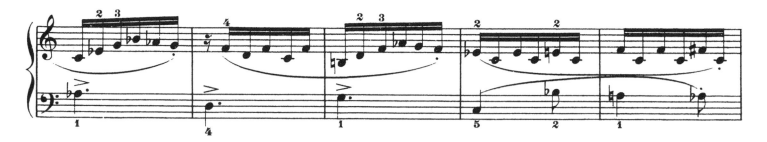

SONATA.

Abbreviations:*) M.T. signifies Main Theme; Ep. Episode; S.T., Sub-Theme; Cl. T., Closing Theme; D.G., Development Group; Md. T. Mid-Theme; R., Return; Tr., Transition; Cod. Codetta; I, II, and III, 1st, 2nd, and 3rd parts of a movement in Song-form (Liedform).

JOSEPH HAYDN.

Allegro con brio.

16.

a) An inverted mordent would appear more appropriate here: b) As at a).

c) When, as in this case, an appoggiatura consists of 2 notes, each at the interval of a second from one of the following principal notes, these latter (here $\frac{c}{a}$) must both be struck after the appoggiatura, whereas the corresponding accompaniment-notes (here E♭ in the bass) enter simultaneously with the appoggiatura.

*) German Equivalents: M.T. signifies Hauptsatz: Ep., Zwischensatz; S.T., Seitensatz; Cl. T. Schlusssatz; D.G., Durchführungssatz; Md. T., Mittelsatz; R., Rückgang; Tr., Übergang; Cod., Anhang; I, II, III,. 1., 2. u. 3. Theil eines liedformigen Satzes.

Var.

11710

S.T. II.

M.T.

a) Make a slight pause after the hold.

Var.

a) After this hold a considerable pause should be made.

Adagio. (♪ = 88.)

M.T.

S.T.

a) Strike the tones in succession from the lowest to the highest, and with a gradual *crescendo*, so that only the highest C attains to an actual *forte*.

b) Keep the accompaniment comparatively subordinate.

11710 c) 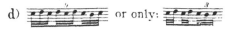 or even only: ▭ d) ▭ or only: ▭

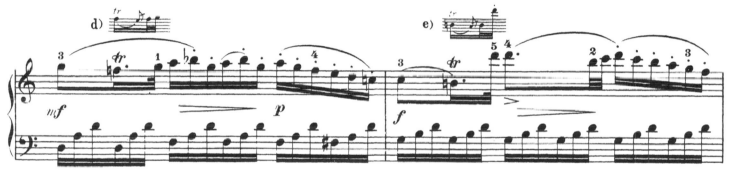

a)  or even only [figure]. b) The accompaniment again comparatively subordinated.

c) As at d) on preceding page.

d) The 32nd-notes F and G coincide with the D in the left hand, and the after-beat E comes immediately before them. [figure] or [figure] e) To be similarly executed

a) Subordinate the accompaniment.

a) Make a considerable pause after the hold.

b) After this hold a very short pause should be made, then attacking the trill instantly:

Prestissimo. ($\bullet$ = 108.)

M.T.

S.T.

a) Cl. T.

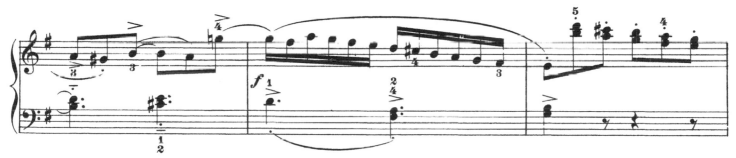

a) Separate from what follows by lifting finger sooner.

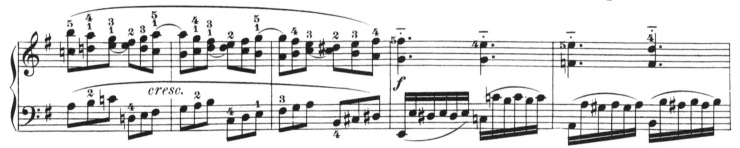

11710

SONATA.

Abbreviations: M. T. signifies Main Theme; Ep., Episode; S. T., Sub-Theme; Cl. T., Closing Theme; D. G., Development-Group; Md. T., Mid-Theme; Cod., Codetta; I., II., III., Ist, 2nd, and 3rd parts of a movement in song form (Liedform).

Revised and fingered by
LUDWIG KLEE.

JOSEPH HAYDN.

Menuetto.

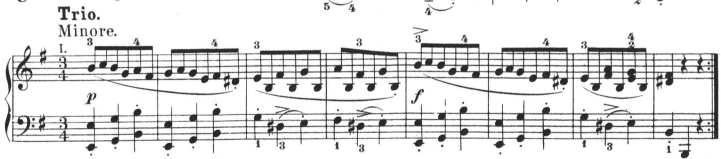

Trio.
Minore.

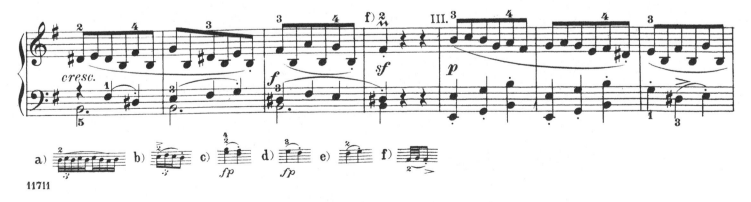

Menuetto D. C.

Finale.
Presto.

11711

SONATA.

Abbreviations: M. T., signifies Main Theme; Ep., Episode; S. T., Sub-Theme; D. G., Development-Group; Cl. T., Closing Theme; Cod., Codetta.

Revised and fingered by *LUDWIG KLEE.*

JOSEPH HAYDN.

Allegro moderato.

18.

Copyright, 1894, by G. Schirmer, Inc.

11712

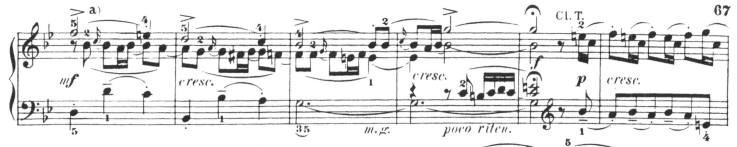

SONATA.

Abbreviations: M. T., signifies Main Theme; Ep., Episode; S. T., Sub-Theme; Cl. T., Closing Theme; D. G., Development-Group; Tr., Transition; I, II, III, 1st, 2nd, and 3rd parts of a movement in song-form (Liedform).

Revised and fingered by
LUDWIG KLEE.

JOSEPH HAYDN.

19.

a) easier:

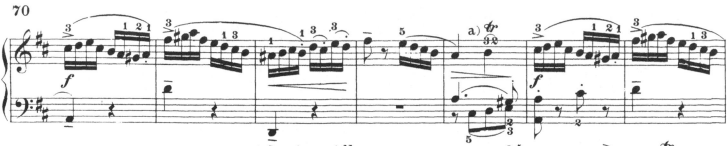

Adagio. Allegro.

11713

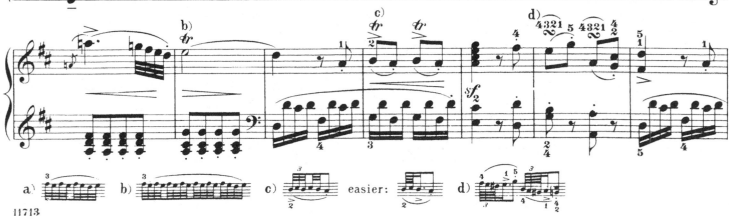

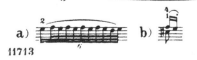

Tempo di Menuetto.

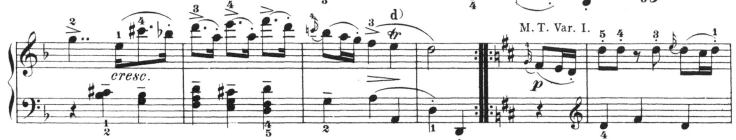

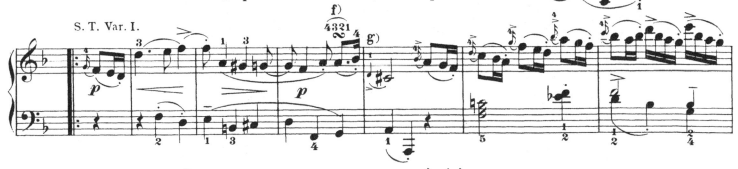

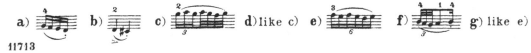

a)

11713

SONATA.

Abbreviations: M. T., signifies Main Theme; Ep., Episode; S. T., Sub-Theme; Cl. T., Closing Theme; D. G., Development-Group; Md. T., Mid-Theme; R., Return; Tr., Transition; Cod., Codetta; I and II, 1st and 2nd parts of a movement in song form (Liedform).

JOSEPH HAYDN.

Allegro moderato. (♩ = 66.)

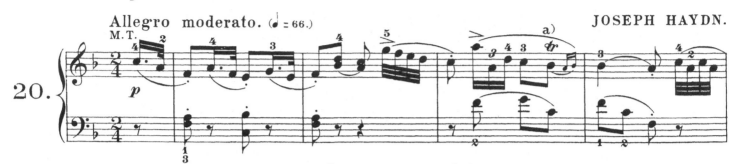

a)  easier:

11714

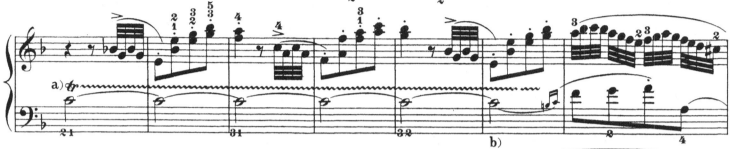

a) The first of the group of grace-notes is to be struck with the A♭ in the left hand.

b) 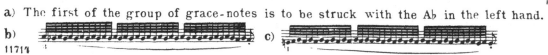 c)

Presto. (♩ = 152)

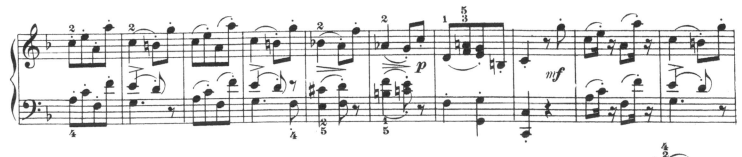

11714

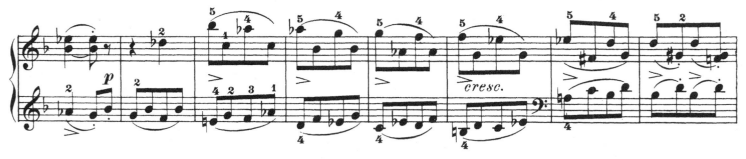

11714